Light From the Living Bible

Perry Tanksley

FLEMING H. REVELL COMPANY
OLD TAPPAN, NEW JERSEY

Scripture quotations in this volume are from The
Living Bible — Tyndale House Publishers, Illi-
nois. Used by permission.

Library of Congress Cataloging in Publication Data

Taylor, Kenneth Nathaniel
    Light from The living Bible.

    1. Bible — Paraphrases, English. I. Tanksley,
Perry, ed. II. Title.
BS550.2.T38 1973b   220.5'2   73-5859
ISBN 0-8007-0597-1

Contents

INTRODUCTION

In this book are selected verses to help light your daily walk. Each verse, and even the phrase at the top of each page, is quoted directly from The Living Bible. Find the help you need easily, and think on it. Key words are set apart for emphasis. Here are some clues on how you might use this book — to read, to think, and to act.

Victory Comes From God — I think the happiest day of my life was when I discovered that God was like Jesus. One day I heard Jesus say, "He who has seen me has seen my Father. I and the Father are one." As a child, I wanted to love God but found myself incapable. Only in Christ and in His revelation of a Christ and in His revelation of a Christlike God could I truly love the Father.

If you would learn to love God, get a proper conception of Him. Behold Jesus breaking bread, healing the sick, fellowshiping with sinners, comforting the lonely and praying for his murderers. All that Jesus was during his earthly ministry, God forever is.

Quit Complaining — Christians express their love in many ways. When parents correct their children, they are expressing their love — even though they often speak in a firm manner. Even a teacher must reprimand with love.

As Christians, we are not asked to speak 'only pleasant positive things. Christian speech sometimes must be disagreeable, but it should be with love.

Be Humble — Take Advice — When one becomes a Christian, he becomes aware not of his brother's sin so much as his own. My flaws, faults, and failures hinder me from helping others. Jesus told us that to help others we should get busy with ourselves. When one is growing closer to God, he is more critical of himself and less critical of others.

To Be My Follower — Do you want a better world? It will have to begin in the home. Would you like to have more truthful neighbors? It must start in the home. You want your community to be safe so you can walk at night? Such a movement must begin in the home. Will this nation survive as the land of the free? It depends on what happens in the home.

Christian Women — A mother must never take lightly the task that is hers. That child entrusted to her care is the hope or curse of the world. The attitude of the adult toward marriage and home is partially determined by the relationship of mother and child. A mother needs the love of God, the grace of the Lord Jesus Christ, and communion with the Holy Spirit.

Partners With Christ — We are saved to witness. We are redeemed to share. We are brought to Christ that we might bring others to Christ. We experience the light of the Gospel that we might become the light of the world.

Be Successful — For a business that honors God, and is run according to Christian principles, the Bible presents some wonderful guidelines for succeeding in business.

Separated From The Lord — Scripture warns that some people are going to be lost from the presence of God. It pains me to know this. It pained God enough to send His only Son to death to save us from eternal separation.

Only God's Will — Don't depend on your conscience to give you proper guidance unless it has been taught from the Word of God.

PERRY TANKSLEY

What a Wonderful God

O LORD, YOU have examined my heart and know everything about me. You know when I sit or stand. When far away you know my every thought. You chart the path ahead of me, and tell me where to stop and rest. Every moment, you know where I am. You know what I am going to say before I even say it. You both precede and follow me, and place your hand of blessing on my head.

This is too glorious, too wonderful to believe! I can *never* be lost to your Spirit! I can *never* get away from my God! If I go up to heaven, you are there; if I go down to the place of the dead, you are there. If I ride the morning winds to the farthest oceans, even there your hand will guide me, your strength will support me. If I try to hide in the darkness, the night becomes light around me. For even darkness cannot hide from God; to you the night shines as bright as day. Darkness and light are both alike to you.

PSALMS 139:1–12

Give Him First Place

What a wonderful God we have — he is the Father of our Lord Jesus Christ, the source of every mercy, and the one who so wonderfully comforts and strengthens us in our hardships and trials. And why does he do this? So that when others are troubled, needing our sympathy and encouragement, we can pass on to them this same help and comfort God has given us.

2 CORINTHIANS 1:3, 4

For he has rescued us out of the darkness and gloom of Satan's kingdom and brought us into the kingdom of his dear Son, who bought our freedom with his blood and forgave us all our sins.

COLOSSIANS 1:13, 14

But I say: Love your *enemies!* Pray for those who *persecute* you! In that way you will be acting as true sons of your Father in heaven. For he gives his sunlight to both the evil and the good, and sends rain on the just and on the unjust too.

MATTHEW 5:44, 45

"So don't worry at all about having enough food and clothing. Why be like the heathen? For they take pride in all these things and are deeply concerned about them. But your heavenly Father already knows perfectly well that you need them, and he will gladly give them to you if you give him first place in your life. . . ."

MATTHEW 6:31–33

Let him have all your worries and cares, for he is always thinking about you and watching everything that concerns you.

1 PETER 5:7

The Lord Is Watching

And if God cares so wonderfully for flowers that are here to-day and gone tomorrow, won't he more surely care for you, O men of little faith?   MATTHEW 6:30

For God sometimes uses sorrow in our lives to help us turn away from sin and seek eternal life. We should never regret his sending it. But the sorrow of the man who is not a Christian is not the sorrow of true repentance and does not prevent eternal death.   2 CORINTHIANS 7:10

After you have suffered a little while, our God, who is full of kindness through Christ, will give you his eternal glory. He personally will come and pick you up, and set you firmly in place, and make you stronger than ever.   1 PETER 5:10

And if you hardhearted, sinful men know how to give good gifts to your children, won't your Father in heaven even more certainly give good gifts to those who ask him for them?   MATTHEW 7:11

Just so, it is not my Father's will that even one of these little ones should perish.   MATTHEW 18:14

For the Lord is watching his children, listening to their prayers; but the Lord's face is hard against those who do evil.   1 PETER 3:12

Notice how God is both so kind and so severe. He is very hard on those who disobey, but very good to you if you continue to love and trust him. But if you don't, you too will be cut off.   ROMANS 11:22

10

Victory Comes From God

For from the very beginning God decided that those who came to him—and all along he knew who would—should become like his Son, so that his Son would be the First, with many brothers. And having chosen us, he called us to come to him; and when we came, he declared us "not guilty," filled us with Christ's goodness, gave us right standing with himself, and promised us his glory.   ROMANS 8:29, 30

We can make our plans, but the final outcome is in God's hands.   PROVERBS 16:1

Look here, you people who say, "Today or tomorrow we are going to such and such a town, stay there a year, and open up a profitable business." How do you know what is going to happen tomorrow? For the length of your lives is as uncertain as the morning fog—now you see it; soon it is gone. What you ought to say is, "If the Lord wants us to, we shall live and do this or that." Otherwise you will be bragging about your own plans, and such self-confidence never pleases God.   JAMES 4:13–16

This plan of mine is not what you would work out, neither are my thoughts the same as yours! For just as the heavens are higher than the earth, so are my ways higher than yours, and my thoughts than yours. ISAIAH 55:8, 9

Go ahead and prepare for the conflict, but victory comes from God. PROVERBS 20:31

Woe to the man who fights with his Creator. Does the pot argue with its maker? Does the clay dispute with him who forms it, saying, "Stop, you're doing it wrong!" or the pot exclaim, "How clumsy can you be!"? Woe to the baby just being born who squalls to his father and mother, "Why have you produced me? Can't you do anything right at all?"

Jehovah, the Holy One of Israel, Israel's Creator, says: What right have you to question what I do? Who are you to command me concerning the work of my hands? ISAIAH 45:9–11

You were there while I was being formed in utter seclusion! You saw me before I was born and scheduled each day of my life before I began to breathe. Every day was recorded in your Book! PSALMS 139:15, 16

12

Jesus Is Lord

YET IT WAS *our* grief he bore, *our* sorrows that weighed him down. And we thought his troubles were a punishment from God, for his *own* sins! But he was wounded and bruised for *our* sins. He was chastised that we might have peace; he was lashed—and we were healed! *We* are the ones who strayed away like sheep! *We*, who left God's paths to follow our own. Yet God laid on *him* the guilt and sins of every one of us!

He was oppressed and he was afflicted, yet he never said a word. He was brought as a lamb to the slaughter, and as a sheep before her shearers is dumb, so he stood silent before the ones condemning him. From prison and trial they led him away to his death. But who among the people of that day realized it was their sins that he was dying for—that he was suffering their punishment? He was buried like a criminal in a rich man's grave; but he had done no wrong, and had never spoken an evil word.   ISAIAH 53:4–9

His Mighty Power and Glory

When we were utterly helpless with no way of escape, Christ came at just the right time and died for us sinners who had no use for him. Even if we were good, we really wouldn't expect anyone to die for us, though, of course, that might be barely possible. But God showed his great love for us by sending Christ to die for us while we were still sinners.   ROMANS 5:6–8

Your attitude should be the kind that was shown us by Jesus Christ, who, though he was God, did not demand and cling to his rights as God, but laid aside his mighty power and glory, taking the disguise of a slave and becoming like men. And he humbled himself even further, going so far as actually to die a criminal's death on a cross.   PHILIPPIANS 2:5–8

And even though Jesus was God's Son, he had to learn from experience what it was like to obey, when obeying meant suffering. It was after he had proved himself perfect in this experience that Jesus became the Giver of eternal salvation to all those who obey him.   HEBREWS 5:8, 9

For God, who said, "Let there be light in the darkness," has made us understand that it is the brightness of his glory that is seen in the face of Jesus Christ.   2 CORINTHIANS 4:6

Christ is the exact likeness of the unseen God. He existed before God made anything at all, and, in fact, Christ himself is the Creator who made everything in heaven and earth, the things we can see and the things we can't; the spirit world with its kings and kingdoms, its rulers and authorities; all were made by Christ for his own use and glory. He was before all else began and it is his power that holds everything together. He is the Head of the body made up of his people—that is, his church—which he began; and he is the Leader of all those who arise from the dead, so that he is first in everything; for God wanted all of himself to be in his Son.   COLOSSIANS 1:15–19

God's Son shines out with God's glory, and all that God's Son is and does marks him as God. He regulates the universe by the mighty power of his command: He is the one who died to cleanse us and clear our record of all sin, and then sat down in highest honor beside the great God of heaven.   HEBREWS 1:3

And Christ became a human being and lived here on earth among us and was full of loving forgiveness and truth. And some of us have seen his glory—the glory of the only Son of the heavenly Father!   JOHN 1:14

Come, Follow Me

Your attitude must be like my own, for I, the Messiah, did not come to be served, but to serve, and to give my life as a ransom for many." MATTHEW 20:28

"There is still one thing you lack," Jesus said. "Sell all you have and give the money to the poor—it will become treasure for you in heaven—and come, follow me."

But when the man heard this he went sadly away, for he was very rich. LUKE 18:22, 23

"Come to me and I will give you rest—all of you who work so hard beneath a heavy yoke. Wear my yoke—for it fits perfectly—and let me teach you; for I am gentle and humble, and you shall find rest for your souls; for I give you only light burdens." MATTHEW 11:28–30

"Don't imagine that I came to bring peace to the earth! No, rather, a sword. I have come to set a man against his father, and a daughter against her mother, and a daughter-in-law against her mother-in-law — a man's worst enemies will be right in his own home! If you love your father and mother more than you love me, you are not worthy of being mine; or if you love your son or daughter more than me, you are not worthy of being mine. If you refuse to take up your cross and follow me, you are not worthy of being mine.

"If you cling to your life, you will lose it; but if you give it up for me, you will save it."   MATTHEW 10:34–39

This suffering is all part of the work God has given you. Christ, who suffered for you, is your example. Follow in his steps: He never sinned, never told a lie, never answered back when insulted; when he suffered he did not threaten to get even; he left his case in the hands of God who always judges fairly. He personally carried the load of our sins in his own body when he died on the cross, so that we can be finished with sin and live a good life from now on. For his wounds have healed ours!

1 PETER 2:21–24

The Wonderful Free Gifts

For it is from God alone that you have your life through Christ Jesus. He showed us God's plan of salvation; he was the one who made us acceptable to God; he made us pure and holy and gave himself to purchase our salvation.

1 CORINTHIANS 1:30

For everything comes from God alone. Everything lives by his power, and everything is for his glory. To him be glory evermore.

ROMANS 11:36

And he guarantees right up to the end that you will be counted free from all sin and guilt on that day when he returns. God will surely do this for you, for he always does just what he says, and he is the one who invited you into this wonderful friendship with his Son, even Christ our Lord.

1 CORINTHIANS 1:8, 9

And God has actually given us his Spirit (not the world's spirit) to tell us about the wonderful free gifts of grace and blessing that God has given us. In telling you about these gifts we have even used the very words given us by the Holy Spirit, not words that we as men might choose. So we use the Holy Spirit's words to explain the Holy Spirit's facts.

1 CORINTHIANS 2:12, 13

He has done this through the death on the cross of his own human body, and now as a result Christ has brought you into the very presence of God, and you are standing there before him with nothing left against you—nothing left that he could even chide you for. . . .

COLOSSIANS 1:22

No Other Way

Jesus told him, "I am the Way — yes, and the Truth and the Life. No one can get to the Father except by means of me." JOHN 14:6

Let God's curses fall on anyone, including myself, who preaches any other way to be saved than the one we told you about; yes, if an angel comes from heaven and preaches any other message, let him be forever cursed. GALATIANS 1:8

"There is salvation in no one else! Under all heaven there is no other name for men to call upon to save them." ACTS 4:12

For they don't understand that Christ has died to make them right with God. Instead they are trying to make themselves good enough to gain God's favor by keeping the Jewish laws and customs, but that is not God's way of salvation. ROMANS 10:3

And what is it that God has said? That he has given us eternal life, and that this life is in his Son. So whoever has God's Son has life; whoever does not have his Son, does not have life.

I have written this to you who believe in the Son of God so that you may know you have eternal life. 1 JOHN 5:11–13

For there is no other way than the one we showed you; you are being fooled by those who twist and change the truth concerning Christ. GALATIANS 1:7

✝

Salvation Is Free

SPRINKLE ME with the cleansing blood and I shall be clean again. Wash me and I shall be whiter than snow. And after you have punished me, give me back my joy again. Don't keep looking at my sins—erase them from your sight. Create in me a new, clean heart, O God, filled with clean thoughts and right desires. Don't toss me aside, banished forever from your presence. Don't take your Holy Spirit from me. Restore to me again the joy of your salvation, and make me willing to obey you. Then I will teach your ways to other sinners, and they—guilty like me—will repent and return to you. Don't sentence me to death. O my God, you alone can rescue me. Then I will sing of your forgiveness, for my lips will be unsealed—oh, how I will praise you.

You don't want penance; if you did, how gladly I would do it! You aren't interested in offerings burned before you on the altar. It is a broken spirit you want—remorse and penitence. A broken and a contrite heart, O God, you will not ignore.   PSALMS 51:7–17

Trust Him

"And all who trust him — God's Son — to save them have eternal life; those who don't believe and obey him shall never see heaven, but the wrath of God remains upon them."

JOHN 3:36

"There is no eternal doom awaiting those who trust him to save them. But those who don't trust him have already been tried and condemned for not believing in the only Son of God."

JOHN 3:18

But we have never turned our backs on God and sealed our fate. No, our faith in him assures our souls' salvation.

HEBREWS 10:39

Because of his kindness you have been saved through trusting Christ. And even trusting is not of yourselves; it too is a gift from God. Salvation is not a reward for the good we have done, so none of us can take any credit for it.

EPHESIANS 2:8, 9

Now we can look forward to the salvation God has promised us. There is no longer any room for doubt, and we can tell others that salvation is ours, for there is no question that he will do what he says.

HEBREWS 10:23

For God in his wisdom saw to it that the world would never find God through human brilliance, and then he stepped in and saved all those who believed his message, which the world calls foolish and silly.

1 CORINTHIANS 1:21

His Unchanging Plan

For it was through reading the Scripture that I came to realize that I could never find God's favor by trying—and failing—to obey the laws. I came to realize that acceptance with God comes by believing in Christ.   GALATIANS 2:19

But God has opened the eyes of those called to salvation, both Jews and Gentiles, to see that Christ is the mighty power of God to save them; Christ himself is the center of God's wise plan for their salvation.   1 CORINTHIANS 1:24

God has told us his secret reason for sending Christ, a plan he decided on in mercy long ago; and this was his purpose: that when the time is ripe he will gather us all together from wherever we are—in heaven or on earth—to be with him in Christ, forever.   EPHESIANS 1:9, 10

For God says, "I will destroy all human plans of salvation no matter how wise they seem to be, and ignore the best ideas of men, even the most brilliant of them."   1 CORINTHIANS 1:19

It is God himself who has made us what we are and given us new lives from Christ Jesus; and long ages ago he planned that we should spend these lives in helping others.
EPHESIANS 2:10

His unchanging plan has always been to adopt us into his own family by sending Jesus Christ to die for us. And he did this because he wanted to!   EPHESIANS 1:5

We Have a Witness to Give

IF THE GOOD NEWS we preach is hidden to anyone, it is hidden from the one who is on the road to eternal death. Satan, who is the god of this evil world, has made him blind, unable to see the glorious light of the Gospel that is shining upon him, or to understand the amazing message we preach about the glory of Christ, who is God. We don't go around preaching about ourselves, but about Christ Jesus as Lord. All we say of ourselves is that we are your slaves because of what Jesus has done for us. For God, who said, "Let there be light in the darkness," has made us understand that it is the brightness of his glory that is seen in the face of Jesus Christ.

But this precious treasure—this light and power that now shine within us—is held in a perishable container, that is, in our weak bodies. Everyone can see that the glorious power within must be from God and is not our own.

2 CORINTHIANS 4:3–7

A Warm Welcome

How true it is, and how I long that everyone should know it, that Christ Jesus came into the world to save sinners — and I was the greatest of them all.   1 TIMOTHY 1:15

For I long to visit you so that I can impart to you the faith that will help your church grow strong in the Lord. Then, too, I need your help, for I want not only to share my faith with you but to be encouraged by yours: Each of us will be a blessing to the other.   ROMANS 1:11, 12

Don't forget about those in jail. Suffer with them as though you were there yourself. Share the sorrow of those being mistreated, for you know what they are going through.   HEBREWS 13:3

Cheerfully share your home with those who need a meal or a place to stay for the night.   1 PETER 4:9

When others are happy, be happy with them. If they are sad, share their sorrow.   ROMANS 12:15

Quietly trust yourself to Christ your Lord and if anybody asks why you believe as you do, be ready to tell him, and do it in a gentle and respectful way.   1 PETER 3:15

Give a warm welcome to any brother who wants to join you, even though his faith is weak. Don't criticize him for having different ideas from yours about what is right and wrong.   ROMANS 14:1

God's Secret Plan

This so-called "foolish" plan of God is far wiser than the wisest plan of the wisest man, and God in his weakness — Christ dying on the cross — is far stronger than any man.

1 CORINTHIANS 1:25

God has sent me to help his church and to tell his secret plan to you Gentiles.

He has kept this secret for centuries and generations past, but now at last it has pleased him to tell it to those who love him and live for him, and the riches and glory of his plan are for you Gentiles too. And this is the secret: *that Christ in your hearts is your only hope of glory.*

COLOSSIANS 1:25–27

Instead, God has deliberately chosen to use ideas the world considers foolish and of little worth in order to shame those people considered by the world as wise and great. He has chosen a plan despised by the world, counted as nothing at all, and used it to bring down to nothing those the world considers great, so that no one anywhere can ever brag in the presence of God.

1 CORINTHIANS 1:27–29

God has given me the wonderful privilege of telling everyone about this plan of his; and he has given me his power and special ability to do it well.

EPHESIANS 3:7

This is what I have asked of God for you: that you will be encouraged and knit together by strong ties of love, and that you will have the rich experience of knowing Christ with real certainty and clear understanding. *For God's secret plan, now at last made known, is Christ himself.*

COLOSSIANS 2:2

28

Tell It Freely

For I am not ashamed of this Good News about Christ. It is God's powerful method of bringing all who believe it to heaven. This message was preached first to the Jews alone, but now everyone is invited to come to God in this same way.

ROMANS 1:16

But thanks be to God! For through what Christ has done, he has triumphed over us so that now wherever we go he uses us to tell others about the Lord and to spread the Gospel like a sweet perfume. 2 CORINTHIANS 2:14

Don't forget to pray for us too, that God will give us many chances to preach the Good News of Christ for which I am here in jail. Pray that I will be bold enough to tell it freely and fully, and make it plain, as, of course, I should. COLOSSIANS 4:3, 4

Only those who, like ourselves, are men of integrity, sent by God, speaking with Christ's power, with God's eye upon us. We are not like those hucksters—and there are many of them—whose idea in getting out the Gospel is to make a good living out of it. 2 CORINTHIANS 2:17

Make the most of your chances to tell others the Good News. Be wise in all your contacts with them. COLOSSIANS 4:5

Just think! Though I did nothing to deserve it, and though I am the most useless Christian there is, yet I was the one chosen for this special joy of telling the Gentiles the Glad News of the endless treasures available to them in Christ. . . .

EPHESIANS 3:8

Love Others

But if instead of showing love among yourselves you are always critical and catty, watch out! Beware of ruining each other.
GALATIANS 5:15

Don't repay evil for evil. Don't snap back at those who say unkind things about you. Instead, pray for God's help for them, for we are to be kind to others, and God will bless us for it.
1 PETER 3:9

Don't just pretend that you love others: really love them. Hate what is wrong. Stand on the side of the good. Love each other with brotherly affection and take delight in honoring each other.
ROMANS 12:9, 10

This will make possible the next step, which is for you to enjoy other people and to like them, and finally you will grow to love them deeply.
2 PETER 1:7

For the whole Law can be summed up in this one command: "Love others as you love yourself."
GALATIANS 5:14

Most important of all, continue to show deep love for each other, for love makes up for many of your faults.
1 PETER 4:8

And we are anxious that you keep right on loving others as long as life lasts, so that you will get your full reward.
HEBREWS 6:11

Then, when that happens, we are able to hold our heads high no matter what happens and know that all is well, for we know how dearly God loves us, and we feel this warm love everywhere within us because God has given us the Holy Spirit to fill our hearts with his love. ROMANS 5:5

Now you can have real love for everyone because your souls have been cleansed from selfishness and hatred when you trusted Christ to save you; so see to it that you really do love each other warmly, with all your hearts. 1 PETER 1:22

In response to all he has done for us, let us outdo each other in being helpful and kind to each other and in doing good. HEBREWS 10:24

If I gave everything I have to poor people, and if I were burned alive for preaching the Gospel but didn't love others, it would be of no value whatever. 1 CORINTHIANS 13:3

What I am eager for is that all the Christians there will be filled with love that comes from pure hearts, and that their minds will be clean and their faith strong. 1 TIMOTHY 1:5

Serve the Lord

Never be lazy in your work but serve the Lord enthusiastically.   ROMANS 12:11

And mark out a straight, smooth path for your feet so that those who follow you, though weak and lame, will not fall and hurt themselves, but become strong.   HEBREWS 12:13

It is God's will that your good lives should silence those who foolishly condemn the Gospel without knowing what it can do for them, having never experienced its power.   1 PETER 2:15

Feed the flock of God; care for it willingly, not grudgingly; not for what you will get out of it, but because you are eager to serve the Lord. Don't be tyrants, but lead them by your good example.
1 PETER 5:2, 3

If you are a preacher, see to it that your sermons are strong and helpful. If God has given you money, be generous in helping others with it. If God has given you administrative ability and put you in charge of the work of others, take the responsibility seriously. Those who offer comfort to the sorrowing should do so with Christian cheer.   ROMANS 12:8

Let everyone be sure that he is doing his very best, for then he will have the personal satisfaction of work well done, and won't need to compare himself with someone else.   GALATIANS 6:4

Living the Life

"THE LAW of Moses says, 'If a man gouges out another's eye, he must pay with his own eye. If a tooth gets knocked out, knock out the tooth of the one who did it.' But I say: Don't resist violence! If you are slapped on one cheek, turn the other too. If you are ordered to court, and your shirt is taken from you, give your coat too. If the military demand that you carry their gear for a mile, carry it two. Give to those who ask, and don't turn away from those who want to borrow.

"There is a saying, 'Love your *friends* and hate your enemies.' But I say: Love your *enemies!* Pray for those who *persecute* you! In that way you will be acting as true sons of your Father in heaven. For he gives his sunlight to both the evil and the good, and sends rain on the just and on the unjust too. If you love only those who love you, what good is that? Even scoundrels do that much. If you are friendly only to your friends, how are you different from anyone else? Even the heathen do that. But you are to be perfect, even as your Father in heaven is perfect."

MATTHEW 5:38–48

Seek To Live

So be careful how you act; these are difficult days. Don't be fools; be wise: make the most of every opportunity you have for doing good. Don't act thoughtlessly, but try to find out and do whatever the Lord wants you to.   EPHESIANS 5:15–17

So get rid of all that is wrong in your life, both inside and outside, and humbly be glad for the wonderful message we have received, for it is able to save our souls as it takes hold of our hearts.   JAMES 1:21

For though once your heart was full of darkness, now it is full of light from the Lord, and your behavior should show it! Because of this light within you, you should do only what is good and right and true.

Learn as you go along what pleases the Lord.
     EPHESIANS 5:8–10

May you always be doing those good, kind things which show that you are a child of God, for this will bring much praise and glory to the Lord.   PHILIPPIANS 1:11

Try to stay out of all quarrels and seek to live a clean and holy life, for one who is not holy will not see the Lord.
     HEBREWS 12:14

If we are living now by the Holy Spirit's power, let us follow the Holy Spirit's leading in every part of our lives.

Then we won't need to look for honors and popularity, which lead to jealousy and hard feelings.   GALATIANS 5:25, 26

Let me say this, then, speaking for the Lord: Live no longer as the unsaved do, for they are blinded and confused. Their closed hearts are full of darkness; they are far away from the life of God because they have shut their minds against him, and they cannot understand his ways. EPHESIANS 4:17, 18

Don't let me hear of your suffering for murdering or stealing or making trouble or being a busybody and prying into other people's affairs. 1 PETER 4:15

We try to live in such a way that no one will ever be offended or kept back from finding the Lord by the way we act, so that no one can find fault with us and blame it on the Lord. 2 CORINTHIANS 6:3

Dear brothers, how can you claim that you belong to the Lord Jesus Christ, the Lord of glory, if you show favoritism to rich people and look down on poor people?

If a man comes into your church dressed in expensive clothes and with valuable gold rings on his fingers, and at the same moment another man comes in who is poor and dressed in threadbare clothes,

And you make a lot of fuss over the rich man and give him the best seat in the house and say to the poor man, "You can stand over there if you like, or else sit on the floor" — well,

This kind of action casts a question mark across your faith — are you really a Christian at all? — and shows that you are guided by wrong motives. JAMES 2:1-4 (REACH OUT)

I would have you learn this great fact: that a life of doing right is the wisest life there is. If you live that kind of life, you'll not limp or stumble as you run. Carry out my instructions; don't forget them, for they will lead you to real living.

PROVERBS 4:11-13

36

Behave Like God's Very Own

So you see, it isn't enough just to have faith. You must also do good to prove that you have it. Faith that doesn't show itself by good works is no faith at all—it is dead and useless.

But someone may well argue, "You say the way to God is by faith alone, plus nothing; well, I say that good works are important too, for without good works you can't prove whether you have faith or not; but anyone can see that I have faith by the way I act."   JAMES 2:17, 18

I can do anything I want to if Christ has not said no, but some of these things aren't good for me. Even if I am allowed to do them, I'll refuse to if I think they might get such a grip on me that I can't easily stop when I want to.   1 CORINTHIANS 6:12

And so we should not be like cringing, fearful slaves, but we should behave like God's very own children, adopted into the bosom of his family, and calling to him, "Father, Father."
                                                              ROMANS 8:15

I advise you to obey only the Holy Spirit's instructions. He will tell you where to go and what to do, and then you won't always be doing the wrong things your evil nature wants you to.
                                                              GALATIANS 5:16

Don't cause the Holy Spirit sorrow by the way you live. Remember, he is the one who marks you to be present on that day when salvation from sin will be complete.   EPHESIANS 4:30

So be careful how you act; these are difficult days. Don't be fools; be wise: make the most of every opportunity you have for doing good.   EPHESIANS 5:15, 16

Away then with sinful, earthly things; deaden the evil desires lurking within you; have nothing to do with sexual sin, impurity, lust and shameful desires; don't worship the good things of life, for that is idolatry. God's terrible anger is upon those who do such things. You used to do them when your life was still part of this world; but now is the time to cast off and throw away all these rotten garments of anger, hatred, cursing, and dirty language.

Don't tell lies to each other; it was your old life with all its wickedness that did that sort of thing; now it is dead and gone.

COLOSSIANS 3:5–9

And now this word to all of you: You should be like one big happy family, full of sympathy toward each other, loving one another with tender hearts and humble minds.   1 PETER 3:8

"Your attitude must be like my own, for I, the Messiah, did not come to be served, but to serve, and to give my life as a ransom for many."   MATTHEW 20:28

Christ Lives in Me

It is quite true that the way to live a godly life is not an easy matter. But the answer lies in Christ, who came to earth as a man, was proved spotless and pure in his Spirit, was served by angels, was preached among the nations, was accepted by men everywhere and was received up again to his glory in heaven.

1 TIMOTHY 3:16

Now I have given up everything else—I have found it to be the only way to really know Christ and to experience the mighty power that brought him back to life again, and to find out what it means to suffer and to die with him. PHILIPPIANS 3:10

I have been crucified with Christ: and I myself no longer live, but Christ lives in me. And the real life I now have within this body is a result of my trusting in the Son of God, who loved me and gave himself for me. GALATIANS 2:20

Then Jesus said to the disciples, "If anyone wants to be a follower of mine, let him deny himself and take up his cross and follow me. For anyone who keeps his life for himself shall lose it; and anyone who loses his life for me shall find it again." MATTHEW 16:24, 25

But to obtain these gifts, you need more than faith; you must also work hard to be good, and even that is not enough. For then you must learn to know God better and discover what he wants you to do. Next, learn to put aside your own desires so that you will become patient and godly, gladly letting God have his way with you. 2 PETER 1:5, 6

39

Be a New and Different Person

Don't be concerned about the outward beauty that depends on jewelry, or beautiful clothes, or hair arrangement. Be beautiful inside, in your hearts, with the lasting charm of a gentle and quiet spirit which is so precious to God. That kind of deep beauty was seen in the saintly women of old, who trusted God and fitted in with their husbands' plans.   1 PETER 3:3–5

You are to live clean, innocent lives as children of God in a dark world full of people who are crooked and stubborn. Shine out among them like beacon lights. . . .   PHILIPPIANS 2:15

But when the Holy Spirit controls our lives he will produce this kind of fruit in us: love, joy, peace, patience, kindness, goodness, faithfulness, gentleness and self-control; and here there is no conflict with Jewish laws.   GALATIANS 5:22, 23

You are living a brand new kind of life that is continually learning more and more of what is right, and trying constantly to be more and more like Christ who created this new life within you.   COLOSSIANS 3:10

Instead, be kind to each other, tenderhearted, forgiving one another, just as God has forgiven you because you belong to Christ.   EPHESIANS 4:32

And now, brothers, as I close this letter let me say this one more thing: Fix your thoughts on what is true and good and right. Think about things that are pure and lovely, and dwell on the fine, good things in others. Think about all you can praise God for and be glad about.   PHILIPPIANS 4:8

Our Unconscious Influence

AND SO, DEAR brothers, I plead with you to give your bodies to God. Let them be a living sacrifice, holy—the kind he can accept. When you think of what he has done for you, is this too much to ask? Don't copy the behavior and customs of this world, but be a new and different person with a fresh newness in all you do and think. Then you will learn from your own experience how his ways will really satisfy you.

As God's messenger I give each of you God's warning: Be honest in your estimate of yourselves, measuring your value by how much faith God has given you. Just as there are many parts to our bodies, so it is with Christ's body. We are all parts of it, and it takes every one of us to make it complete, for we each have different work to do. So we belong to each other, and each needs all the others. ROMANS 12:1–5

Never Avenge Yourselves

Stop being mean, bad-tempered and angry. Quarreling, harsh words, and dislike of others should have no place in your lives.

EPHESIANS 4:31

. . . never haughty or selfish or rude. Love does not demand its own way. It is not irritable or touchy. It does not hold grudges and will hardly even notice when others do it wrong.

1 CORINTHIANS 13:5

Dear brothers, don't ever forget that it is best to listen much, speak little, and not become angry; for anger doesn't make us good, as God demands that we must be.

JAMES 1:19, 20

If you are angry, don't sin by nursing your grudge. Don't let the sun go down with you still angry — get over it quickly; for when you are angry you give a mighty foothold to the devil.

EPHESIANS 4:26, 27

If someone mistreats you because you are a Christian, don't curse him; pray that God will bless him.

ROMANS 12:14

Dear friends, never avenge yourselves. Leave that to God, for he has said that he will repay those who deserve it. [Don't take the law into your own hands.]

Instead, feed your enemy if he is hungry. If he is thirsty give him something to drink and you will be "heaping coals of fire on his head." In other words, he will feel ashamed of himself for what he has done to you. Don't let evil get the upper hand but conquer evil by doing good.

ROMANS 12:19–21

Show Forth the Power

If anyone defiles and spoils God's home, God will destroy him. For God's home is holy and clean, and you are that home.

1 CORINTHIANS 3:17

Haven't you yet learned that your body is the home of the Holy Spirit God gave you, and that he lives within you? Your own body does not belong to you.

For God has bought you with a great price. So use every part of your body to give glory back to God, because he owns it.

1 CORINTHIANS 6:19, 20

And so, dear brothers, I plead with you to give your bodies to God. Let them be a living sacrifice, holy — the kind he can accept. When you think of what he has done for you, is this too much to ask?

ROMANS 12:1

But this precious treasure — this light and power that now shine within us — is held in a perishable container, that is, in our weak bodies. Everyone can see that the glorious power within must be from God and is not our own.

2 CORINTHIANS 4:7

Do not let any part of your bodies become tools of wickedness, to be used for sinning; but give yourselves completely to God — every part of you — for you are back from death and you want to be tools in the hands of God, to be used for his good purposes.

ROMANS 6:13

Yes, we live under constant danger to our lives because we serve the Lord, but this gives us constant opportunities to show forth the power of Jesus Christ within our dying bodies.

2 CORINTHIANS 4:11

For the Glory of God

If I can thank God for the food and enjoy it, why let someone spoil everything just because he thinks I am wrong? Well, I'll tell you why. It is because you must do everything for the glory of God, even your eating and drinking. So don't be a stumbling block to anyone, whether they are Jews or Gentiles or Christians.
1 CORINTHIANS 10:30–32

So don't let anyone criticize you for what you eat or drink; or for not celebrating Jewish holidays and feasts or new moon ceremonies or Sabbaths. For these were only temporary rules that ended when Christ came. They were only shadows of the real thing—of Christ himself.
COLOSSIANS 2:16

So do not be attracted by strange, new ideas. Your spiritual strength comes as a gift from God, not from ceremonial rules about eating certain foods—a method which, by the way, hasn't helped those who have tried it!
HEBREWS 13:9

Don't undo the work of God for a chunk of meat. Remember, there is nothing wrong with the meat, but it is wrong to eat it if it makes another stumble. The right thing to do is to quit eating meat or drinking wine or doing anything else that offends your brother or makes him sin.
ROMANS 14:20, 21

For instance, take the matter of eating. God has given us an appetite for food and stomachs to digest it. But that doesn't mean we should eat more than we need. Don't think of eating as important, because some day God will do away with both stomachs and food.
But sexual sin is never right: our bodies were not made for that, but for the Lord, and the Lord wants to fill our bodies with himself.
1 CORINTHIANS 6:13

45

Carousing and Drinking

"Watch out! Don't let my sudden coming catch you un-
awares; don't let me find you living in careless ease, carousing
and drinking, and occupied with the problems of this life, like all
the rest of the world."   LUKE 21:34, 35

Wine gives false courage; hard liquor leads to brawls; what
fools men are to let it master them, making them reel drunkenly
down the street!   PROVERBS 20:1

Be decent and true in everything you do so that all can approve
your behavior. Don't spend your time in wild parties and getting
drunk or in adultery and lust, or fighting, or jealousy.
                                                           ROMANS 13:13

A man who loves pleasure becomes poor; wine and luxury are
not the way to riches!   PROVERBS 21:17

Woe to you who get up early in the morning to go on long
drinking bouts that last till late at night = woe to you drunken
bums. You furnish lovely music at your grand parties; the
orchestras are superb! But for the Lord you have no thought
or care.   ISAIAH 5:11, 12

Our Speech Betrays Us

MEN HAVE TRAINED, or can train, every kind of animal or bird that lives and every kind of reptile and fish, but no human being can tame the tongue. It is always ready to pour out its deadly poison. Sometimes it praises our heavenly Father, and sometimes it breaks out into curses against men who are made like God. And so blessing and cursing come pouring out of the same mouth. Dear brothers, surely this is not right! Does a spring of water bubble out first with fresh water and then with bitter water? Can you pick olives from a fig tree, or figs from a grape vine? No, and you can't draw fresh water from a salty pool.

If you are wise, live a life of steady goodness, so that only good deeds will pour forth. And if you don't brag about them, then you will be truly wise! And by all means don't brag about being wise and good if you are bitter and jealous and selfish; that is the worst sort of lie.

JAMES 3:7–14

Say Only What Is Good

Stop lying to each other; tell the truth, for we are parts of each other and when we lie to each other we are hurting ourselves.   EPHESIANS 4:25

We don't go around preaching about ourselves, but about Christ Jesus as Lord. All we say of ourselves is that we are your slaves because of what Jesus has done for us.
                                                              2 CORINTHIANS 4:5

Don't use bad language. Say only what is good and helpful to those you are talking to, and what will give them a blessing.
                                                              EPHESIANS 4:29

Anyone who says he is a Christian but doesn't control his sharp tongue is just fooling himself, and his religion isn't worth much.
                                                              JAMES 1:26

Dirty stories, foul talk and coarse jokes — these are not for you. Instead, remind each other of God's goodness and be thankful.
                                                              EPHESIANS 5:4

Don't quarrel with anyone. Be at peace with everyone, just as much as possible.   ROMANS 12:18

Talk with each other much about the Lord, quoting psalms and hymns and singing sacred songs, making music in your hearts to the Lord.   EPHESIANS 5:19

Don't criticize, and then you won't be criticized! For others will treat you as you treat them.   MATTHEW 7:1, 2

Quit Complaining

I said to myself, **I'm going to quit complaining!** I'll keep quiet, especially when the ungodly are around me.

PSALMS 39:1

In everything you do, stay away from complaining and arguing, so that no one can speak a word of blame against you. You are to live clean, innocent lives as children of God in a dark world full of people who are crooked and stubborn. Shine out among them like beacon lights.

PHILIPPIANS 2:14, 15

And don't murmur against God and his dealings with you, as some of them did, for that is why God sent his Angel to destroy them.

1 CORINTHIANS 10:10

The people were soon complaining about all their misfortunes, and the Lord heard them. His anger flared out against them because of their complaints, so the fire of the Lord began destroying those at the far end of the camp.

NUMBERS 11:1

"He will bring the people of the world before him in judgment, to receive just punishment, and to prove the terrible things they have done in rebellion against God, revealing all they have said against him." These men are constant gripers, never satisfied, doing whatever evil they feel like; they are loudmouthed "show-offs," and when they show respect for others, it is only to get something from them in return.   JUDE 1:15, 16

Why then should we, mere humans as we are, murmur and complain when punished for our sins? Let us examine ourselves instead, and repent and turn again to the Lord.

LAMENTATIONS 3:39, 40

If anyone can control his tongue, it proves that he has perfect control over himself in every other way. We can make a large horse turn around and go wherever we want by means of a small bit in his mouth. And a tiny rudder makes a huge ship turn wherever the pilot wants it to go, even though the winds are strong.

So also the tongue is a small thing, but what enormous damage it can do. A great forest can be set on fire by one tiny spark. And the tongue is a flame of fire. It is full of wickedness, and poisons every part of the body. And the tongue is set on fire by hell itself, and can turn our whole lives into a blazing flame of destruction and disaster.   - .   JAMES 3:2–6

Be Humble-Take Advice

A fool is quick-tempered; a wise man stays cool when insulted.
PROVERBS 12:16

Pride leads to arguments; be humble, take advice and become wise.
PROVERBS 13:10

To learn, you must want to be taught. To refuse reproof is stupid.
PROVERBS 12:1

Be happy if you are cursed and insulted for being a Christian, for when that happens the Spirit of God will come upon you with great glory. Don't let me hear of your suffering for murdering or stealing or making trouble or being a busybody and prying into other people's affairs.
1 PETER 4:14, 15

"When you are reviled and persecuted and lied about because you are my followers—wonderful! Be *happy* about it! Be *very glad!* for a *tremendous reward* awaits you up in heaven. And remember, the ancient prophets were persecuted too."
MATTHEW 5:11

What I meant was that you are not to keep company with anyone who claims to be a brother Christian but indulges in sexual sins, or is greedy, or is a swindler, or worships idols, or is a drunkard, or abusive. Don't even eat lunch with such a person.

1 CORINTHIANS 5:11

Don't repay evil for evil. Don't snap back at those who say unkind things about you. Instead, pray for God's help for them, for we are to be kind to others, and God will bless us for it.

1 PETER 3:9

"Don't criticize, and then you won't be criticized. For others will treat you as you treat them."

MATTHEW 7:1

If you profit from constructive criticism you will be elected to the wise men's hall of fame. But to reject criticism is to harm yourself and your own best interests.

PROVERBS 15:31, 32

Don't criticize and speak evil about each other, dear brothers. If you do, you will be fighting against God's law of loving one another, declaring it is wrong. But your job is not to decide whether this law is right or wrong, but to obey it. Only he who made the law can rightly judge among us. He alone decides to save us or destroy. So what right do you have to judge or criticize others?

JAMES 4:11

Look After Each Other

Work happily together. Don't try to act big. Don't try to get into the good graces of important people, but enjoy the company of ordinary folks. And don't think you know it all!

ROMANS 12:16

And now this word to all of you: You should be like one big happy family, full of sympathy toward each other, loving one another with tender hearts and humble minds. 1 PETER 3:8

Look after each other so that not one of you will fail to find God's best blessings. Watch out that no bitterness takes root among you, for as it springs up it causes deep trouble, hurting many in their spiritual lives. HEBREWS 12:15

Pay all your debts except the debt of love for others — never finish paying that! For if you love them, you will be obeying all of God's laws, fulfilling all his requirements. ROMANS 13:8

Since you have been chosen by God who has given you this new kind of life, and because of his deep love and concern for you, you should practice tenderhearted mercy and kindness to others. Don't worry about making a good impression on them but be ready to suffer quietly and patiently.

COLOSSIANS 3:12

"If a brother sins against you, go to him privately and confront him with his fault. If he listens and confesses it, you have won back a brother." MATTHEW 18:15

No Place Like Home

SHE IS a woman of strength and dignity, and has no fear of old age. When she speaks, her words are wise, and kindness is the rule for everything she says. She watches carefully all that goes on throughout her household, and is never lazy. Her children stand and bless her; so does her husband. He praises her with these words: "There are many fine women in the world, but you are the best of them all!"

Charm can be deceptive and beauty doesn't last, but a woman who fears and reverences God shall be greatly praised. Praise her for the many fine things she does. These good deeds of hers shall bring her honor and recognition from even the leaders of the nations.

PROVERBS 31:25–31

Be Loving and Kind

Honor your marriage and its vows, and be pure; for God will surely punish all those who are immoral or commit adultery.
HEBREWS 13:4

You husbands must be careful of your wives, being thoughtful of their needs and honoring them as the weaker sex. Remember that you and your wife are partners in receiving God's blessings, and if you don't treat her as you should, your prayers will not get ready answers.
1 PETER 3:7

You wives, submit yourselves to your husbands. for that is what the Lord has planned for you. And you husbands must be loving and kind to your wives and not bitter against them, nor harsh.
COLOSSIANS 3:18, 19

So again I say, a man must love his wife as a part of himself; and the wife must see to it that she deeply respects her husband — obeying, praising and honoring him.
EPHESIANS 5:33

Wives, fit in with your husbands' plans: for then if they refuse to listen when you talk to them about the Lord, they will be won by your respectful, pure behavior. Your godly lives will speak to them better than any words.
1 PETER 3:1

So you wives must willingly obey your husbands in everything, just as the church obeys Christ.
And you husbands, show the same kind of love to your wives as Christ showed to the church when he died for her.
EPHESIANS 5:24, 25

To Be My Follower

Only fools refuse to be taught. Listen to your father and mother. What you learn from them will stand you in good stead; it will gain you many honors.   PROVERBS 1:8, 9

Children, obey your parents; this is the right thing to do because God has placed them in authority over you. Honor your father and mother. This is the first of God's Ten Commandments that ends with a promise. And this is the promise: that if you honor your father and mother, yours will be a long life, full of blessing.   EPHESIANS 6:1–3

"Don't you read the Scriptures?" he replied. "In them it is written that at the beginning God created man and woman, and that a man should leave his father and mother, and be forever united to his wife. The two shall become one — no longer two, but one! And no man may divorce what God has joined together."
          MATTHEW 19:4–6

"Honor your father and mother, that you may have a long, good life in the land the Lord your God will give you."
          EXODUS 20:12

58

"For instance, Moses gave you this law from God: 'Honor your father and mother.' And he said that anyone who speaks against his father or mother must die. But you say it is perfectly all right for a man to disregard his needy parents, telling them, 'Sorry, I can't help you! For I have given to God what I could have given to you.' And so you break the law of God in order to protect your man-made tradition. And this is only one example. There are many, many others."

MARK 7:10–13

Great crowds were following him. He turned around and addressed them as follows: "Anyone who wants to be my follower must love me far more than he does his own father, mother, wife, children, brothers, or sisters — yes, more than his own life — otherwise he cannot be my disciple. And no one can be my disciple who does not carry his own cross and follow me."

LUKE 14:25–27

"But watch out! Be very careful never to forget what you have seen God doing for you. May his miracles have a deep and permanent effect upon your lives! Tell your children and your grandchildren about the glorious miracles he did."

DEUTERONOMY 4:9

Always Expect the Best of Him

And now a word to you parents. Don't keep on scolding and nagging your children, making them angry and resentful. Rather, bring them up with the loving discipline the Lord himself approves, with suggestions and godly advice.   EPHESIANS 6:4

If you love someone you will be loyal to him no matter what the cost. You will always believe in him, always expect the best of him, and always stand your ground in defending him.
                                         1 CORINTHIANS 13:7

Children, obey your parents; this is the right thing to do because God has placed them in authority over you.
Honor your father and mother. This is the first of God's Ten Commandments that ends with a promise. And this is the promise: that if you honor your father and mother, yours will be a long life, full of blessing.   EPHESIANS 6:1-3

And you must think constantly about these commandments I am giving you today. You must teach them to your children and talk about them when you are at home or out for a walk; at bedtime and the first thing in the morning. Tie them on your finger, wear them on your forehead, and write them on the doorposts of your house!   DEUTERONOMY 6:6-9

And now this word to all of you: You should be like one big happy family, full of sympathy toward each other, loving one another with tender hearts and humble minds.   1 PETER 3:8

But anyone who won't care for his own relatives when they need help, especially those living in his own family, has no right to say he is a Christian. Such a person is worse than the heathen.
                                              1 TIMOTHY 5:8

Christian Women

And the women should be the same way, quiet and sensible in manner and clothing. Christian women should be noticed for being kind and good, not for the way they fix their hair or because of their jewels or fancy clothes.   1 TIMOTHY 2:9, 10

Wives, fit in with your husbands' plans; for then if they refuse to listen when you talk to them about the Lord, they will be won by your respectful, pure behavior. Your godly lives will speak to them better than any words.

Don't be concerned about the outward beauty that depends on jewelry, or beautiful clothes, or hair arrangement. Be beautiful inside, in your hearts, with the lasting charm of a gentle and quiet spirit which is so precious to God.   1 PETER 3:1–4

If you can find a truly good wife, she is worth more than precious gems! Her husband can trust her, and she will richly satisfy his needs.   PROVERBS 31:10

Charm can be deceptive and beauty doesn't last, but a woman who fears and reverences God shall be greatly praised. Praise her for the many fine things she does. These good deeds of hers shall bring her honor and recognition from even the leaders of the nations.   PROVERBS 31:30, 31

Teach the older women to be quiet and respectful in everything they do. They must not go around speaking evil of others and must not be heavy drinkers, but they should be teachers of goodness. These older women must train the younger women to live quietly, to love their husbands and their children, and to be sensible and clean minded, spending their time in their own homes, being kind and obedient to their husbands, so that the Christian faith can't be spoken against by those who know them.

Titus 2:3–5

She is a woman of strength and dignity, and has no fear of old age. When she speaks, her words are wise, and kindness is the rule for everything she says. She watches carefully all that goes on throughout her household, and is never lazy. Her children stand and bless her; so does her husband. He praises her with these words: "There are many fine women in the world, but you are the best of them all!"

Proverbs 31:25–29

Some Have Never Heard

BUT HOW shall they ask him to save them unless they believe in him? And how can they believe in him if they have never heard about him? And how can they hear about him unless someone tells them? And how will anyone go and tell them unless someone sends him? That is what the Scriptures are talking about when they say, "How beautiful are the feet of those who preach the Gospel of peace with God and bring glad tidings of good things." In other words, how welcome are those who come preaching God's Good News!

But not everyone who hears the Good News has welcomed it, for Isaiah the prophet said, "Lord, who has believed me when I told them?" Yet faith comes from listening to this Good News—the Good News about Christ.

ROMANS 10:14–17

This Sacred Trust

We don't go around preaching about ourselves, but about Christ Jesus as Lord. All we say of ourselves is that we are your slaves because of what Jesus has done for us.

2 CORINTHIANS 4:5

For I am not ashamed of this Good News about Christ. It is God's powerful method of bringing all who believe it to heaven. This message was preached first to the Jews alone, but now everyone is invited to come to God in this same way.

ROMANS 1:16

And so I solemnly urge you before God and before Christ Jesus—who will some day judge the living and the dead when he appears to set up his kingdom—to preach the Word of God urgently at all times, whenever you get the chance, in season and out, when it is convenient and when it is not. Correct and rebuke your people when they need it, encourage them to do right, and all the time be feeding them patiently with God's Word.

For there is going to come a time when people won't listen to the truth, but will go around looking for teachers who will tell them just what they want to hear. 2 TIMOTHY 4:1–3

For Christ didn't send me to baptize, but to preach the Gospel; and even my preaching sounds poor, for I do not fill my sermons with profound words and high sounding ideas, for fear of diluting the mighty power there is in the simple message of the cross of Christ. 1 CORINTHIANS 1:17

For just preaching the Gospel isn't any special credit to me — I couldn't keep from preaching it if I wanted to. I would be utterly miserable. Woe unto me if I don't.

If I were volunteering my services of my own free will, then the Lord would give me a special reward; but that is not the situation, for God has picked me out and given me this sacred trust and I have no choice.   1 CORINTHIANS 9:16, 17

I left you there on the island of Crete so that you could do whatever was needed to help strengthen each of its churches, and I asked you to appoint pastors in every city who would follow the instructions I gave you. The men you choose must be well thought of for their good lives; they must have only one wife and their children must love the Lord and not have a reputation for being wild or disobedient to their parents.

These pastors must be men of blameless lives because they are God's ministers. They must not be proud or impatient; they must not be drunkards or fighters or greedy for money.
                                            TITUS 1:5–7

Partners With Christ

Praise the Lord if you are punished for doing right!
Of course, you get no credit for being patient if you are beaten
for doing wrong; but if you do right and suffer for it, and are patient beneath the blows, God is well pleased.

1 PETER 2:19, 20

We can rejoice, too, when we run into problems and trials for
we know that they are good for us—they help us learn to be patient.

ROMANS 5:3

"For when he punishes you, it proves that he loves you. When
he whips you it proves you are really his child."
Let God train you, for he is doing what any loving father does
for his children. Whoever heard of a son who was never cor-
rected?

HEBREWS 12:6, 7

For to you has been given the privilege not only of trusting
him but also of suffering for him.

PHILIPPIANS 1:29

We are pressed on every side by troubles, but not crushed and
broken. We are perplexed because we don't know why things
happen as they do, but we don't give up and quit.

2 CORINTHIANS 4:8

And since we are his children, we will share his treasures—for
all God gives to his Son Jesus is now ours too. But if we are to
share his glory, we must also share his suffering.

ROMANS 8:17

Dear friends, don't be bewildered or surprised when you go through the fiery trials ahead, for this is no strange, unusual thing that is going to happen to you. Instead, be really glad — because these trials will make you partners with Christ in his suffering, and afterwards you will have the wonderful joy of sharing his glory in that coming day when it will be displayed.

1 PETER 4:12, 13

And I want you to know this, dear brothers. Everything that has happened to me here has been a great boost in getting out the Good News concerning Christ. For everyone around here, including all the soldiers over at the barracks, knows that I am in chains simply because I am a Christian.

PHILIPPIANS 1:12, 13

So be truly glad! There is wonderful joy ahead, even though the going is rough for a while down here.   1 PETER 1:6

Build Each Other Up

Share each other's troubles and problems, and so obey our Lord's command. If anyone thinks he is too great to stoop to this, he is fooling himself. He is really a nobody.

GALATIANS 6:2, 3

In this way aim for harmony in the church and try to build each other up.

ROMANS 14:19

But, dear brothers, I beg you in the name of the Lord Jesus Christ to stop arguing among yourselves. Let there be real harmony so that there won't be splits in the church. I plead with you to be of one mind, united in thought and purpose.

1 CORINTHIANS 1:10

And why worry about a speck in the eye of a brother when you have a board in your own? Should you say, "Friend, let me help you get that speck out of your eye," when you can't even see because of the board in your own? Hypocrite! First get rid of the board. Then you can see to help your brother.

MATTHEW 7:3–5

Yes, each of us will give an account of himself to God. So don't criticize each other any more. Try instead to live in such a way that you will never make your brother stumble by letting him see you doing something he thinks is wrong.

ROMANS 14:12, 13

Dear brothers, if a Christian is overcome by some sin, you who are godly should gently and humbly help him back onto the right path, remembering that next time it might be one of you who is in the wrong.

GALATIANS 6:1

The Rich Treasures Within

You can detect them by the way they act, just as you can identify a tree by its fruit. You need never confuse grapevines with thorn bushes! Or figs with thistles! Different kinds of fruit trees can quickly be identified by examining their fruit. A variety that produces delicious fruit never produces an inedible kind! And a tree producing an inedible kind can't produce what is good! So the trees having the inedible fruit are chopped down and thrown on the fire. Yes, the way to identify a tree or a person is by the kind of fruit produced.   MATTHEW 7:16–20

So stop evaluating Christians by what the world thinks about them or by what they seem to be like on the outside. Once I mistakenly thought of Christ that way, merely as a human being like myself. How differently I feel now!

2 CORINTHIANS 5:16

For I have told you often before, and I say it again now with tears in my eyes, there are many who walk along the Christian road who are really enemies of the cross of Christ.

Their future is eternal loss, for their god is their appetite: they are proud of what they should be ashamed of; and all they think about is this life here on earth.   PHILIPPIANS 3:18, 19

A good man's speech reveals the rich treasures within him. An evil-hearted man is filled with venom, and his speech reveals it.

MATTHEW 12:35

God Has Exalted Us

WHEN I LOOK UP into the night skies and see the work of your fingers—the moon and the stars you have made—I cannot understand how you can bother with mere puny man, to pay any attention to him! And yet you have made him only a little lower than the angels, and placed a crown of glory and honor upon his head.

You have put him in charge of everything you made; everything is put under his authority: all sheep and oxen, and wild animals too, the birds and fish, and all the life in the sea. O Jehovah, our Lord, the majesty and glory of your name fills the earth.   PSALMS 8:3–9

A Fresh Newness

For because of our faith, he has brought us into this place of highest privilege where we now stand, and we confidently and joyfully look forward to actually becoming all that God has had in mind for us to be.   ROMANS 5:2

When someone becomes a Christian he becomes a brand new person inside. He is not the same any more. A new life has begun!
2 CORINTHIANS 5:17

Then throw off your old evil nature—the old you that was a partner in your evil ways—rotten through and through, full of lust and sham.
Now your attitudes and thoughts must all be constantly changing for the better. Yes, you must be a new and different person, holy and good. Clothe yourself with this new nature.
EPHESIANS 4:22–24

No, dear brothers, I am still not all I should be but I am bringing all my energies to bear on this one thing: Forgetting the past and looking forward to what lies ahead, I strain to reach the end of the race and receive the prize for which God is calling us up to heaven because of what Christ Jesus did for us.
PHILIPPIANS 3:13, 14

You are living a brand new kind of life that is continually learning more and more of what is right, and trying constantly to be more and more like Christ who created this new life within you.   COLOSSIANS 3:10

Don't copy the behavior and customs of this world, but be a new and different person with a fresh newness in all you do and think. Then you will learn from your own experience how his ways will really satisfy you.   ROMANS 12:2

72

To Be the Greatest

"The more lowly your service to others, the greater you are. To be the greatest, be a servant. But those who think themselves great shall be disappointed and humbled; and those who humble themselves shall be exalted."   MATTHEW 23:11, 12

Jesus called a small child over to him and set the little fellow down among them, and said, "Unless you turn to God from your sins and become as little children, you will never get into the Kingdom of Heaven. Therefore anyone who humbles himself as this little child, is the greatest in the Kingdom of Heaven."
MATTHEW 18:2–4

Don't be conceited, sure of your own wisdom. Instead, trust and reverence the Lord, and turn your back on evil; when you do that, then you will be given renewed health and vitality.
PROVERBS 3:7, 8

"But among you it is quite different. Anyone wanting to be a leader among you must be your servant. And if you want to be right at the top, you must serve like a slave."
MATTHEW 20:26, 27

What are you so puffed up about? What do you have that God hasn't given you? And if all you have is from God, why act as though you are so great, and as though you have accomplished something on your own?   1 CORINTHIANS 4:7

Put God First

If you must choose, take a good name rather than great riches; for to be held in loving esteem is better than silver and gold.   PROVERBS 22:1

There are three things that remain — faith, hope, and love — and the greatest of these is love.   1 CORINTHIANS 13:13

Don't be selfish; don't live to make a good impression on others. Be humble, thinking of others as better than yourself. Don't just think about your own affairs, but be interested in others, too, and in what they are doing.   PHILIPPIANS 2:3, 4

If you want favor with both God and man, and a reputation for good judgment and common sense, then trust the Lord completely; don't ever trust yourself. In everything you do, put God first, and he will direct you and crown your efforts with success.   PROVERBS 3:4–6

Some rich people are poor, and some poor people have great wealth!   PROVERBS 13:7

Because You Are Young

Children are a gift from God; they are his reward.
PSALMS 127:3

It is good for a young man to be under discipline, for it causes him to sit apart in silence beneath the Lord's demands, to lie face downward in the dust; then at last there is hope for him.
LAMENTATIONS 3:27–29

Teach a child to choose the right path, and when he is older he will remain upon it.
PROVERBS 22:6

Don't let anyone think little of you because you are young. Be their ideal; let them follow the way you teach and live; be a pattern for them in your love, your faith, and your clean thoughts.
1 TIMOTHY 4:12

The character of even a child can be known by the way he acts — whether what he does is pure and right.
PROVERBS 20:11

Don't let the excitement of being young cause you to forget about your Creator. Honor him in your youth before the evil years come — when you'll no longer enjoy living. It will be too late then to try to remember him, when the sun and light and moon and stars are dim to your old eyes, and there is no silver lining left among your clouds.
ECCLESIASTES 12:1, 2

Forgive Us Our Trespasses

O LOVING AND kind God, have mercy.

Have pity upon me and take away the awful stain of my transgressions. Oh, wash me, cleanse me from this guilt. Let me be pure again. For I admit my shameful deed — it haunts me day and night. It is against you and you alone I sinned, and did this terrible thing. You saw it all, and your sentence against me is just. But I was born a sinner, yes, from the moment my mother conceived me. You deserve honesty from the heart; yes, utter sincerity and truthfulness. Oh, give me this wisdom.   PSALMS 51:1–6

MASS. D.P.W.
TRAFFIC DIV.

Apart From Christ

And it is a sin against Christ to sin against your brother by encouraging him to do something he thinks is wrong.

1 CORINTHIANS 8:12

If anyone sins deliberately by rejecting the Savior after knowing the truth of forgiveness, this sin is not covered by Christ's death; there is no way to get rid of it.

There will be nothing to look forward to but the terrible punishment of God's awful anger which will consume all his enemies.

HEBREWS 10:26, 27

Giving preferred treatment to rich people is a clear case of selling one's soul for a piece of bread.   PROVERBS 28:21

That is why I say to run from sex sin. No other sin affects the body as this one does. When you sin this sin it is against your own body.   1 CORINTHIANS 6:18

The night is far gone, the day of his return will soon be here. So quit the evil deeds of darkness and put on the armor of right living, as we who live in the daylight should! Be decent and true in everything you do so that all can approve your behavior. Don't spend your time in wild parties and getting drunk or in adultery and lust, or fighting, or jealousy. But ask the Lord Jesus Christ to help you live as you should, and don't make plans to enjoy evil.

ROMANS 13:12-14

Dear brothers, you are only visitors here. Since your real home is in heaven I beg you to keep away from the evil pleasures of this world; they are not for you, for they fight against your very souls.   1 PETER 2:11

For instance, take the matter of eating. God has given us an appetite for food and stomachs to digest it. But that doesn't mean we should eat more than we need. Don't think of eating as important, because some day God will do away with both stomachs and food.

But sexual sin is never right: our bodies were not made for that, but for the Lord, and the Lord wants to fill our bodies with himself. 1 CORINTHIANS 6:13

The Lord despises every kind of cheating.

PROVERBS 20:10

Remember that in those days you were living utterly apart from Christ; you were enemies of God's children and he had promised you no help. You were lost, without God, without hope.

EPHESIANS 2:12

And you won't be spending the rest of your life chasing after evil desires, but will be anxious to do the will of God. You have had enough in the past of the evil things the godless enjoy — sex sin, lust, getting drunk, wild parties, drinking bouts, and the worship of idols, and other terrible sins. 1 PETER 4:2, 3

Every one has turned away; all have gone wrong. No one anywhere has kept on doing what is right; not one.

ROMANS 3:12

So get rid of your feelings of hatred. Don't just pretend to be good! Be done with dishonesty and jealousy and talking about others behind their backs. 1 PETER 2:1

Unfit

My little children, I am telling you this so that you will stay away from sin. But if you sin, there is someone to plead for you before the Father. His name is Jesus Christ, the one who is all that is good and who pleases God completely. He is the one who took God's wrath against our sins upon himself, and brought us into fellowship with God; and he is the forgiveness for our sins, and not only ours but all the world's.   1 JOHN 2:1, 2

In a race, everyone runs but only one person gets first prize. So run your race to win. To win the contest you must deny yourselves many things that would keep you from doing your best. An athlete goes to all this trouble just to win a blue ribbon or a silver cup, but we do it for a heavenly reward that never disappears. So I run straight to the goal with purpose in every step. I fight to win. I'm not just shadowboxing or playing around. Like an athlete I punish my body, treating it roughly, training it to do what it should, not what it wants to. Otherwise I fear that after enlisting others for the race, I myself might be declared unfit and ordered to stand aside.   1 CORINTHIANS 9:24–27

A Wandering Soul

There is no use trying to bring you back to the Lord again if you have once understood the Good News and tasted for yourself the good things of heaven and shared in the Holy Spirit, and know how good the Word of God is, and felt the mighty powers of the world to come, and then have turned against God. You cannot bring yourself to repent again if you have nailed the Son of God to the cross again by rejecting him, holding him up to mocking and to public shame.   HEBREWS 6:4–6

Dear brothers, if anyone has slipped away from God and no longer trusts the Lord, and someone helps him understand the Truth again, that person who brings him back to God will have saved a wandering soul from death, bringing about the forgiveness of his many sins.   JAMES 5:19, 20

Do not let this happy trust in the Lord die away, no matter what happens. Remember your reward! You need to keep on patiently doing God's will if you want him to do for you all that he has promised. His coming will not be delayed much longer. And those whose faith has made them good in God's sight must live by faith, trusting him in everything. Otherwise, if they shrink back, God will have no pleasure in them.   HEBREWS 10:35–38

Wrong Inclinations

But remember this — the wrong desires that come into your life aren't anything new and different. Many others have faced exactly the same problems before you. And no temptation is irresistible. You can trust God to keep the temptation from becoming so strong that you can't stand up against it, for he has promised this and will do what he says. He will show you how to escape temptation's power so that you can bear up patiently against it.   1 CORINTHIANS 10:13, 14

When you are guided by the Holy Spirit you need no longer force yourself to obey Jewish laws.

But when you follow your own wrong inclinations your lives will produce these evil results: impure thoughts, eagerness for lustful pleasure, idolatry, spiritism (that is, encouraging the activity of demons), hatred and fighting, jealousy and anger, constant effort to get the best for yourself, complaints and criticisms, the feeling that everyone else is wrong except those in your own little group — and there will be wrong doctrine, envy, murder, drunkenness, wild parties, and all that sort of thing. Let me tell you again as I have before, that anyone living that sort of life will not inherit the kingdom of God.   GALATIANS 5:18–21

"But if your eye is clouded with evil thoughts and desires, you are in deep spiritual darkness. And oh, how deep that darkness can be!"   MATTHEW 6:23

Obey God's Laws

Those laws are good when used as God intended.

But they were not made for us, whom God has saved; they are for sinners who hate God, have rebellious hearts, curse and swear, attack their fathers and mothers, and murder. Yes, these laws are made to identify as sinners all who are immoral and impure: homosexuals, kidnappers, liars, and all others who do things that contradict the glorious Good News of our blessed God, whose messenger I am. 1 Timothy 1:8-11

Well then, am I suggesting that these laws of God are evil? Of course not! No, the law is not sinful but it was the law that showed me my sin. I would never have known the sin in my heart—the evil desires that are hidden there—if the law had not said, "You must not have evil desires in your heart."

Romans 7:7

Consequently, it is clear that no one can ever win God's favor by trying to keep the Jewish laws, because God has said that the only way we can be right in his sight is by faith. As the prophet Habakkuk says it, "The man who finds life will find it through trusting God." How different from this way of faith is the way of law which says that a man is saved by obeying every law of God, without one slip. Galatians 3:11, 12

The Ten Commandments were given so that all could see the extent of their failure to obey God's laws. But the more we see our sinfulness, the more we see God's abounding grace forgiving us. Romans 5:20

Stand Firm

Happy is the man who doesn't give in and do wrong when he is tempted, for afterwards he will get as his reward the crown of life that God has promised those who love him. And remember, when someone wants to do wrong it is never God who is tempting him, for 'God never wants to do wrong and never tempts anyone else to do it. Temptation is the pull of man's own evil thoughts and wishes. These evil thoughts lead to evil actions and afterwards to the death penalty from God.   JAMES 1:12–15

So be truly glad! There is wonderful joy ahead, even though the going is rough for a while down here.

These trials are only to test your faith, to see whether or not it is strong and pure. It is being tested as fire tests gold and purifies it — and your faith is far more precious to God than mere gold; so if your faith remains strong after being tried in the test tube of fiery trials, it will bring you much praise and glory and honor on the day of his return.   1 PETER 1:6, 7

Last of all I want to remind you that your strength must come from the Lord's mighty power within you. Put on all of God's armor so that you will be able to stand safe against all strategies and tricks of Satan. For we are not fighting against people made of flesh and blood, but against persons without bodies — the evil rulers of the unseen world, those mighty satanic beings and great evil princes of darkness who rule this world; and against huge numbers of wicked spirits in the spirit world.

EPHESIANS 6:10–12

Be careful—watch out for attacks from Satan, your great enemy. He prowls around like a hungry, roaring lion, looking for some victim to tear apart. Stand firm when he attacks. Trust the Lord; and remember that other Christians all around the world are going through these sufferings too.   1 PETER 5:8, 9

But this precious treasure—this light and power that now shine within us—is held in a perishable container, that is, in our weak bodies. Everyone can see that the glorious power within must be from God and is not our own.

We are pressed on every side by troubles, but not crushed and broken. We are perplexed because we don't know why things happen as they do, but we don't give up and quit. We are hunted down, but God never abandons us. We get knocked down, but we get up again and keep going. These bodies of ours are constantly facing death just as Jesus did; so it is clear to all that it is only the living Christ within [who keeps us safe].

Yes, we live under constant danger to our lives because we serve the Lord, but this gives us constant opportunities to show forth the power of Jesus Christ within our dying bodies.

2 CORINTHIANS 4:7–11

And if we think that our present service for him is hard, just remember that some day we are going to sit with him and rule with him. But if we give up when we suffer, and turn against Christ, then he must turn against us. Even when we are too weak to have any faith left, he remains faithful to us and will help us, for he cannot disown us who are part of himself, and he will always carry out his promises to us.   2 TIMOTHY 2:12, 13

Dear brothers, is your life full of difficulties and temptations? Then be happy, for when the way is rough, your patience has a chance to grow. So let it grow, and don't try to squirm out of your problems. For when your patience is finally in full bloom, then you will be ready for anything, strong in character, full and complete.   JAMES 1:2–4

Life Can Be Beautiful

THE LORD is my light and my salvation; whom shall I fear? When evil men come to destroy me, they will stumble and fall! Yes, though a mighty army marches against me, my heart shall know no fear! I am confident that God will save me.

The one thing I want from God, the thing I seek most of all, is the privilege of meditating in his Temple, living in his presence every day of my life, delighting in his incomparable perfections and glory. There I'll be when troubles come. He will hide me. He will set me on a high rock out of reach of all my enemies. Then I will bring him sacrifices and sing his praises with much joy. Listen to my pleading, Lord! Be merciful and send the help I need.

PSALMS 27:1–7

Sunshine in Your Soul

Happy are all who perfectly follow the laws of God. **Happy are all who search for God,** and always do his will, rejecting compromise with evil, and walking only in his paths.

PSALMS 119:1–3

Happy are those whose hearts are pure, for they shall see God. **Happy are those who strive for peace** – they shall be called the sons of God. MATTHEW 5:8, 9

For the Scriptures tell us that no one who believes in Christ **will ever be disappointed.** ROMANS 10:11

If you want a happy, good life, keep control of your tongue, and guard your lips from telling lies. 1 PETER 3:10

For, dear brothers, you have been given freedom: not freedom to do wrong, but **freedom to love and serve each other.**
For the whole Law can be summed up in this one command: "Love others as you love yourself." GALATIANS 5:13, 14

Follow the steps of the godly instead, and stay on the right path, for **only good men enjoy life to the full;** evil men lose the good things they might have had, and they themselves shall be destroyed. PROVERBS 2:20–22

"If your eye is pure, **there will be sunshine in your soul."**

MATTHEW 6:22

Always Be Thankful

Always be joyful. Always keep on praying. No matter what happens, always be thankful, for this is God's will for you who belong to Christ Jesus. 1 THESSALONIANS 5:16–18

If you have good eyesight and good hearing, thank God who gave them to you. PROVERBS 20:12

For all the animals of field and forest are mine! The cattle on a thousand hills! And all the birds upon the mountains! If I were hungry, I would not mention it to you—for all the world is mine, and everything in it. No, I don't need your sacrifices of flesh and blood. What I want from you is your true thanks; I want your promises fulfilled. *I want you to trust me in your times of trouble, so I can rescue you, and you can give me glory.*

PSALMS 50:10–15

With Jesus' help we will continually offer our sacrifice of praise to God by telling others of the glory of his name. Don't forget to do good and to share what you have with those in need, for such sacrifices are very pleasing to him. HEBREWS 13:15, 16

Don't Worry

Don't worry about anything; instead, pray about everything; tell God your needs and don't forget to thank him for his answers. If you do this you will experience God's peace, which is far more wonderful than the human mind can understand. His peace will keep your thoughts and your hearts quiet and at rest as you trust in Christ Jesus. PHILIPPIANS 4:6, 7

Let heaven fill your thoughts; don't spend your time worrying about things down here. COLOSSIANS 3:2

"So my counsel is: Don't worry about *things* — food, drink, money, and clothes. For you already have life and a body — and they are far more important than what to eat and wear. MATTHEW 6:25

Since you have been chosen by God who has given you this new kind of life, and because of his deep love and concern for you, you should practice tenderhearted mercy and kindness to others. Don't worry about making a good impression on them but be ready to suffer quietly and patiently. COLOSSIANS 3:12

Everyone else seems to be worrying about his own plans and not those of Jesus Christ. PHILIPPIANS 2:21

"So don't be anxious about tomorrow. God will take care of your tomorrow too. Live one day at a time. MATTHEW 6:34

His Brand

And anyone who gives up his home, brothers, sisters, father, mother, wife, children, or property, to follow me, shall receive a hundred times as much in return, and shall have eternal life.

MATTHEW 19:29

For if we are faithful to the end, trusting God just as we did when we first became Christians, we will share in all that belongs to Christ. HEBREWS 3:14

So that anyone who believes in me will have eternal life. For God loved the world so much that he gave his only Son so that anyone who believes in him shall not perish but have eternal life. God did not send his Son into the world to condemn it, but to save it. JOHN 3:15–17

"So be prepared, for you don't know what day your Lord is coming.

"Just as a man can prevent trouble from thieves by keeping watch for them, so you can avoid trouble by always being ready for my unannounced return." MATTHEW 24:42, 44

But you are not like that. You are controlled by your new nature if you have the Spirit of God living in you. (And remember that if anyone doesn't have the Spirit of Christ living in him, he is not a Christian at all.) ROMANS 8:9

He has put his brand upon us—his mark of ownership—and given us his Holy Spirit in our hearts as guarantee that we belong to him, and as the first installment of all that he is going to give us. 2 CORINTHIANS 1:22

Stand at Your Post of Duty

STAND STEADY, and don't be afraid of suffering for the Lord. Bring others to Christ. Leave nothing undone that you ought to do.

I say this because I won't be around to help you very much longer. My time has almost run out. Very soon now I will be on my way to heaven. I have fought long and hard for my Lord, and through it all I have kept true to him. And now the time has come for me to stop fighting and rest. In heaven a crown is waiting for me which the Lord, the righteous Judge, will give me on that great day of his return. And not just to me, but to all those whose lives show that they are eagerly looking forward to his coming back again.

2 TIMOTHY 4:5–8

Be Successful

Any enterprise is built by wise planning, becomes strong through common sense, and profits wonderfully by keeping abreast of the facts.   PROVERBS 24:3, 4

"You must be impartial in judgment. Use accurate measurements—lengths, weights, and volumes—and give full measure, for I am Jehovah your God who brought you from the land of Egypt."
                                                      LEVITICUS 19:35, 36

Never be lazy in your work but serve the Lord enthusiastically.
                                                      ROMANS 12:11

Lazy men are soon poor; hard workers get rich.
                                                      PROVERBS 10:4

So I saw that there is nothing better for men than that they should be happy in their work, for that is what they are here for, and no one can bring them back to life to enjoy what will be in the future, so let them enjoy it now.   ECCLESIASTES 3:22

A lazy man won't even dress the game he gets while hunting, but the diligent man makes good use of everything he finds.
                                                      PROVERBS 12:27

Always remember that it is the Lord your God who gives you power to become rich, and he does it to fulfill his promise to your ancestors. DEUTERONOMY 8:18

Do you know a hard-working man? He shall be successful and stand before kings! PROVERBS 22:29

Again I looked throughout the earth and saw that the swiftest person does not always win the race, nor the strongest man the battle, and that wise men are often poor, and skillful men are not necessarily famous; but it is all by chance, by happening to be at the right place at the right time. A man never knows when he is going to run into bad luck. He is like a fish caught in a net, or a bird caught in a snare. ECCLESIASTES 9:11, 12

A man who refuses to admit his mistakes can never be successful. But if he confesses and forsakes them, he gets another chance. PROVERBS 28:13

You Have Robbed Me

"Will a man rob God? Surely not! And yet you have robbed me.

" 'What do you mean? When did we ever rob you?'

"You have robbed me of the tithes and offerings due to me. And so the awesome curse of God is cursing you, for your whole nation has been robbing me. Bring all the tithes into the storehouse so that there will be food enough in my Temple; if you do, I will open up the windows of heaven for you and pour out a blessing so great you won't have room enough to take it in!

"Try it! Let me prove it to you! Your crops will be large, for I will guard them from insects and plagues. Your grapes won't shrivel away before they ripen," says the Lord of Hosts. "And all nations will call you blessed, for you will be a land sparkling with happiness. These are the promises of the Lord of Hosts."

MALACHI 3:8–12

Honor the Lord by giving him the first part of all your income, and he will fill your barns with wheat and barley and overflow your wine vats with the finest wines.   PROVERBS 3:9, 10

97

Honor the Government

Watching their opportunity, they sent secret agents pretending to be honest men. They said to Jesus, "Sir, we know what an honest teacher you are. You always tell the truth and don't budge an inch in the face of what others think, but teach the ways of God. Now tell us—is it right to pay taxes to the Roman government or not?"

He saw through their trickery and said, "Show me a coin. Whose portrait is this on it? And whose name?"

They replied, "Caesar's—the Roman emperor's."

He said, "Then give the emperor all that is his—and give to God all that is his!"

Thus their attempt to outwit him before the people failed; and marveling at his answer, they were silent.   LUKE 20:20–26

Obey the government, for God is the one who has put it there. There is no government anywhere that God has not placed in power. So those who refuse to obey the laws of the land are refusing to obey God, and punishment will follow. For the policeman does not frighten people who are doing right; but those doing evil will always fear him. So if you don't want to be afraid, keep the laws and you will get along well.   ROMANS 13:1–3

Show respect for everyone. Love Christians everywhere. Fear God and honor the government.   1 PETER 2:17

The policeman is sent by God to help you. But if you are doing something wrong, of course you should be afraid, for he will have you punished. He is sent by God for that very purpose. Obey the laws, then, for two reasons: first, to keep from being punished, and second, just because you know you should.

ROMANS 13:4, 5

Be careful how you behave among your unsaved neighbors; for then, even if they are suspicious of you and talk against you, they will end up praising God for your good works when Christ returns. For the Lord's sake, obey every law of your government: those of the king as head of the state, and those of the king's officers, for he has sent them to punish all who do wrong, and to honor those who do right.   1 PETER 2:12–14

Pay your taxes too, for these same two reasons. For government workers need to be paid so that they can keep on doing God's work, serving you. Pay everyone whatever he ought to have: pay your taxes and import duties gladly, obey those over you, and give honor and respect to all those to whom it is due.

ROMANS 13:6, 7

A Rich Man

But as for me, my contentment is not in wealth but in seeing you and knowing all is well between us. And when I awake in heaven, I will be fully satisfied, for I will see you face to face.

PSALMS 17:15

Then Jesus said to his disciples, "It is almost impossible for a rich man to get into the Kingdom of Heaven. I say it again—it is easier for a camel to go through the eye of a needle than for a rich man to enter the Kingdom of God!"

MATTHEW 19:23, 24

Stay away from the love of money, be satisfied with what you have. For God has said, "I will never, *never* fail you nor forsake you."

HEBREWS 13:5

But a rich man should be glad that his riches mean nothing to the Lord, for he will soon be gone, like a flower that has lost its beauty and fades away, withered—killed by the scorching summer sun. So it is with rich men. They will soon die and leave behind all their busy activities.

JAMES 1:10, 11

Tell them to use their money to do good. They should be rich in good works and should give happily to those in need, always being ready to share with others whatever God has given them. By doing this they will be storing up real treasure for themselves in heaven—it is the only safe investment for eternity! And they will be living a fruitful Christian life down here as well.

1 TIMOTHY 6:18, 19

To Love Christ Supremely

LOVE is very patient and kind, never jealous or envious, never boastful or proud, never haughty or selfish or rude. Love does not demand its own way. It is not irritable or touchy. It does not hold grudges and will hardly even notice when others do it wrong. It is never glad about injustice, but rejoices whenever truth wins out. If you love someone you will be loyal to him no matter what the cost. You will always believe in him, always expect the best of him, and always stand your ground in defending him.

All the special gifts and powers from God will someday come to an end, but love goes on forever. Someday prophecy, and speaking in unknown languages, and special knowledge — these gifts will disappear.   1 CORINTHIANS 13:4–8

Not Seeing Him

"Because of your little faith," Jesus told them. "For if you had faith even as small as a tiny mustard seed you could say to this mountain, 'Move!' and it would go far away. Nothing would be impossible. But this kind of demon won't leave unless you have prayed and gone without food."

MATTHEW 17:20, 21

Are there still some among you who hold that "only believing" is enough? Believing in one God? Well, remember that the devils believe this too—so strongly that they tremble in terror!

Fool! When will you ever learn that "believing" is useless without *doing* what God wants you to? Faith that does not result in good deeds is not real faith.

JAMES 2:19, 20

And now just as you trusted Christ to save you, trust him, too, for each day's problems; live in vital union with him. Let your roots grow down into him and draw up nourishment from him. See that you go on growing in the Lord, and become strong and vigorous in the truth you were taught. Let your lives overflow with joy and thanksgiving for all he has done.

COLOSSIANS 2:6, 7

You love him even though you have never seen him; though not seeing him, you trust him; and even now you are happy with the inexpressible joy that comes from heaven itself.

1 PETER 1:8

103

Be a Partner

If young toughs tell you, "Come and join us" – turn your back on them! "We'll hide and rob and kill," they say. "Good or bad, we'll treat them all alike. And the loot we'll get! All kinds of stuff! Come on, throw in your lot with us; we'll split with you in equal shares."

Don't do it, son! Stay far from men like that, for crime is their way of life, and murder is their specialty.

PROVERBS 1:10–16

Don't be teamed with those who do not love the Lord, for what do the people of God have in common with the people of sin? How can light live with darkness? And what harmony can there be between Christ and the devil? How can a Christian be a partner with one who doesn't believe? And what union can there be between God's temple and idols? For you are God's temple, the home of the living God, and God has said of you, "I will live in them and walk among them, and I will be their God and they shall be my people." That is why the Lord has said, "Leave them; separate yourselves from them; don't touch their filthy things, and I will welcome you, and be a Father to you, and you will be my sons and daughters."

2 CORINTHIANS 6:14–18

Judged and Punished

"But if the man begins to think, 'My Lord won't be back for a long time,' and begins to whip the men and women he is supposed to protect, and to spend his time at drinking parties and in drunkenness—well, his master will return without notice and remove him from his position of trust and assign him to the place of the unfaithful. He will be severely punished, for though he knew his duty he refused to do it.

"But anyone who is not aware that he is doing wrong will be punished only lightly. Much is required from those to whom much is given, for their responsibility is greater."

LUKE 12:45–48

Young man, do not resent it when God chastens and corrects you, for his punishment is proof of his love. Just as a father punishes a son he delights in to make him better, so the Lord corrects you.   PROVERBS 3:11, 12

But if you carefully examine yourselves before eating you will not need to be judged and punished. Yet, when we are judged and punished by the Lord, it is so that we will not be condemned with the rest of the world.   1 CORINTHIANS 11:31, 32

Shallow Answers

These wicked men, so proud and haughty, seem to think that God is dead. They wouldn't think of looking for him!

PSALMS 10:4

And now there is one more thing to say before I end this letter. Stay away from those who cause divisions and are upsetting people's faith, teaching things about Christ that are contrary to what you have been taught. Such teachers are not working for our Lord Jesus, but only want gain for themselves. They are good speakers, and simple-minded people are often fooled by them.

ROMANS 16:17, 18

So what about these wise men, these scholars, these brilliant debaters of this world's great affairs? God has made them all look foolish, and shown their wisdom to be useless nonsense. For God in his wisdom saw to it that the world would never find God through human brilliance, and then he stepped in and saved all those who believed his message, which the world calls foolish and silly.

1 CORINTHIANS 1:20, 21

That man is a fool who says to himself, "There is no God!" Anyone who talks like that is warped and evil and cannot really be a good person at all.

PSALMS 14:1

Sailing on Uncharted Seas

AND THEN there are the sailors sailing the seven seas, plying the trade routes of the world. They, too, observe the power of God in action. He calls to the storm winds; the waves rise high. Their ships are tossed to the heavens and sink again to the depths; the sailors cringe in terror. They reel and stagger like drunkards and are at their wit's end. Then they cry to the Lord in their trouble, and he saves them. He calms the storm and stills the waves. What a blessing is that stillness, as he brings them safely into harbor! Oh, that these men would praise the Lord for his lovingkindness and for all of his wonderful deeds! Let them praise him publicly before the congregation, and before the leaders of the nation.

PSALMS 107:23–32

Never Right

For instance, take the matter of eating. God has given us an appetite for food and stomachs to digest it. But that doesn't mean we should eat more than we need. Don't think of eating as important, because some day God will do away with both stomachs and food.

But sexual sin is never right: our bodies were not made for that, but for the Lord, and the Lord wants to fill our bodies with himself.   1 CORINTHIANS 6:13

And you won't be spending the rest of your life chasing after evil desires, but will be anxious to do the will of God. You have had enough in the past of the evil things the godless enjoy — sex sin, lust, getting drunk, wild parties, drinking bouts, and the worship of idols, and other terrible sins.   1 PETER 4:2, 3

Don't you know that those doing such things have no share in the Kingdom of God? Don't fool yourselves. Those who live immoral lives, who are idol worshipers, adulterers or homosexuals — will have no share in his kingdom. Neither will thieves or greedy people, drunkards, slandermongers, or robbers.
                                                  1 CORINTHIANS 6:9, 10

But if you give yourself to the Lord, you and Christ are joined together as one person.
That is why I say to run from sex sin. No other sin affects the body as this one does. When you sin this sin it is against your own body. Haven't you yet learned that your body is the home of the Holy Spirit God gave you, and that he lives within you? Your own body does not belong to you.

For God has bought you with a great price. So use every part of your body to give glory back to God, because he owns it.
                                                 1 CORINTHIANS 6:17–20

Share the Sorrow

You are a poor specimen if you can't stand the pressure of adversity. PROVERBS 24:10

Don't forget about those in jail. Suffer with them as though you were there yourself. Share the sorrow of those being mistreated, for you know what they are going through.
HEBREWS 13:3

Dear friends, don't be bewildered or surprised when you go through the fiery trials ahead, for this is no strange, unusual thing that is going to happen to you. Instead, be really glad— because these trials will make you partners with Christ in his suffering, and afterwards you will have the wonderful joy of sharing his glory in that coming day when it will be displayed.

Be happy if you are cursed and insulted for being a Christian, for when that happens the Spirit of God will come upon you with great glory. 1 PETER 4:12–14

See the way God does things and fall into line. Don't fight the facts of nature. Enjoy prosperity whenever you can, and when hard times strike, realize that God gives one as well as the other —so that everyone will realize that nothing is certain in this life.
ECCLESIASTES 7:13, 14

Keep on Patiently

So if you are suffering according to God's will, keep on doing what is right and trust yourself to the God who made you, for he will never fail you.   1 PETER 4:19

We are pressed on every side by troubles, but not crushed and broken. We are perplexed because we don't know why things happen as they do, but we don't give up and quit.
                    2 CORINTHIANS 4:8

Be careful — watch out for attacks from Satan, your great enemy. He prowls around like a hungry, roaring lion, looking for some victim to tear apart. Stand firm when he attacks. Trust the Lord; and remember that other Christians all around the world are going through these sufferings too.   1 PETER 5:8, 9

Do not let this happy trust in the Lord die away, no matter what happens. Remember your reward! You need to keep on patiently doing God's will if you want him to do for you all that he has promised.   HEBREWS 10:35, 36

So my dear brothers, since future victory is sure, be strong and steady, always abounding in the Lord's work, for you know that nothing you do for the Lord is ever wasted as it would be if there were no resurrection.   1 CORINTHIANS 15:58

And let us not get tired of doing what is right, for after a while we will reap a harvest of blessing if we don't get discouraged and give up.   GALATIANS 6:9

That is why we never give up. Though our bodies are dying, our inner strength in the Lord is growing every day.
                    2 CORINTHIANS 4:16

An Account of Himself

You will be judged on whether or not you are doing what Christ wants you to. So watch what you do and what you think; for there will be no mercy to those who have shown no mercy. But if you have been merciful, then God's mercy toward you will win out over his judgment against you.   JAMES 2:12, 13

There is going to come a time of testing at Christ's Judgment Day to see what kind of material each builder has used. Everyone's work will be put through the fire so that all can see whether or not it keeps its value, and what was really accomplished. Then every workman who has built on the foundation with the right materials, and whose work still stands, will get his pay. But if the house he has built burns up, he will have a great loss. He himself will be saved, but like a man escaping through a wall of flames.   1 CORINTHIANS 3:13-15

Don't be misled; remember that you can't ignore God and get away with it: a man will always reap just the kind of crop he sows! If he sows to please his own wrong desires, he will be planting seeds of evil and he will surely reap a harvest of spiritual decay and death; but if he plants the good things of the Spirit, he will reap the everlasting life which the Holy Spirit gives him.   GALATIANS 6:7, 8

Dear friends, never avenge yourselves. Leave that to God, for he has said that he will repay those who deserve it. [Don't take the law into your own hands.]   ROMANS 12:19

112

There's More to Come

"SEE, I AM coming soon, and my reward is with me, to repay everyone according to the deeds he has done. I am the A and the Z, the Beginning and the End, the First and Last. Blessed forever are all who are washing their robes, to have the right to enter in through the gates of the city, and to eat the fruit from the Tree of Life."   REVELATION 22:12–14

Look Forward Eagerly

Then, knowing what lies ahead for you, you won't become bored with being a Christian, nor become spiritually dull and indifferent, but you will be anxious to follow the example of those who receive all that God has promised them because of their strong faith and patience.   HEBREWS 6:12

So we do not look at what we can see right now, the troubles all around us, but we look forward to the joys in heaven which we have not yet seen. The troubles will soon be over, but the joys to come will last forever.   2 CORINTHIANS 4:18

In the same way, we can see and understand only a little about God now, as if we were peering at his reflection in a poor mirror; but someday we are going to see him in his completeness, face to face. Now all that I know is hazy and blurred, but then I will see everything clearly, just as clearly as God sees into my heart right now.   1 CORINTHIANS 13:12

For this world is not our home; we are looking forward to our everlasting home in heaven.   HEBREWS 13:14

For we know that when this tent we live in now is taken down — when we die and leave these bodies — we will have wonderful new bodies in heaven, homes that will be ours forevermore, made for us by God himself, and not by human hands. How weary we grow of our present bodies. That is why we look forward eagerly to the day when we shall have heavenly bodies which we shall put on like new clothes.
                              2 CORINTHIANS 5:1, 2

Separated From the Lord

For the wages of sin is death, but the free gift of God is eternal life through Jesus Christ our Lord.   ROMANS 6:23

And so I would say to you who are suffering, God will give you rest along with us when the Lord Jesus appears suddenly from heaven in flaming fire with his mighty angels, bringing judgment on those who do not wish to know God, and who refuse to accept his plan to save them through our Lord Jesus Christ. They will be punished in everlasting hell, forever separated from the Lord, never to see the glory of his power, when he comes to receive praise and admiration because of all he has done for his people, his saints. And you will be among those praising him, because you have believed what we told you about him.

2 THESSALONIANS 1:7–10

"But if you are evil and say to yourself, 'My Lord won't be coming for a while,' and begin oppressing your fellow servants, partying and getting drunk, your Lord will arrive unannounced and unexpected, and severely whip you and send you off to the judgment of the hypocrites; there will be weeping and gnashing of teeth."   MATTHEW 24:48–51

The Backslider

Dear brothers, if anyone has slipped away from God and no longer trusts the Lord, and someone helps him understand the Truth again, that person who brings him back to God will have saved a wandering soul from death, bringing about the forgiveness of his many sins.   JAMES 5:19, 20

The backslider gets bored with himself; the godly man's life is exciting.   PROVERBS 14:14

Your own wickedness will punish you. You will see what an evil, bitter thing it is to rebel against the Lord your God, fearlessly forsaking him, says the Lord, the God of Hosts. Long ago you shook off my yoke and broke away from my ties. Defiant, you would not obey me. On every hill and under every tree you've bowed low before idols.   JEREMIAH 2:19, 20

Dear brothers, if a Christian is overcome by some sin, you who are godly should gently and humbly help him back onto the right path, remembering that next time it might be one of you who is in the wrong.   GALATIANS 6:1

Grow in His Grace

Search me, O God, and know my heart; test my thoughts. Point out anything you find in me that makes you sad, and lead me along the path of everlasting life. PSALMS 139:23, 24

Since we have such a huge crowd of men of faith watching us from the grandstands, let us strip off anything that slows us down or holds us back, and especially those sins that wrap themselves so tightly around our feet and trip us up; and let us run with patience the particular race that God has set before us. HEBREWS 12:1

If you have tasted the Lord's goodness and kindness, cry for more, as a baby cries for milk. Eat God's Word—read it, think about it—and grow strong in the Lord and be saved. 1 PETER 2:2, 3 (REACH OUT)

Bodily exercise is all right, but spiritual exercise is much more important and is a tonic for all you do. So exercise yourself spiritually and practice being a better Christian, because that will help you not only now in this life, but in the next life too. 1 TIMOTHY 4:8

Let us not neglect our church duties and meetings, as some people do, but encourage and warn each other, especially now that the day of his coming back again is drawing near. HEBREWS 10:25

I don't mean to say I am perfect. I haven't learned all I should even yet, but I keep working toward that day when I will finally be all that Christ saved me for and wants me to be. PHILIPPIANS 3:12

Remember: God Is Holy

LORD, WHO MAY go and find refuge and shelter in your tabernacle up on your holy hill?

Anyone who leads a blameless life and is truly sincere. Anyone who refuses to slander others, does not listen to gossip, never harms his neighbor, speaks out against sin, criticizes those committing it, commends the faithful followers of the Lord, keeps a promise even if it ruins him, does not crush his debtors with high interest rates, and refuses to testify against the innocent despite the bribes offered him—such a man shall stand firm forever.   PSALMS 15:1–5

Many Times a Day

Stand before the Lord in awe, and do not sin against him. Lie quietly upon your bed in silent meditation.   PSALMS 4:4

"Constantly remind the people about these laws, and you yourself must think about them every day and every night so that you will be sure to obey all of them. For only then will you succeed. Yes, be bold and strong! Banish fear and doubt! For remember, the Lord your God is with you wherever you go."

JOSHUA 1:8, 9

How precious it is, Lord, to realize that you are thinking about me constantly! I can't even count how many times a day your thoughts turn towards me. And when I waken in the morning, you are still thinking of me!   PSALMS 139:17, 18

But when you pray, go away by yourself, all alone, and shut the door behind you and pray to your Father secretly, and your Father, who knows your secrets, will reward you.

MATTHEW 6:6

Don't Be Impatient

My God, my God, why have you forsaken me? Why do you refuse to help me or even to listen to my groans? Day and night I keep on weeping, crying for your help, but there is no reply—for *you are holy.*   PSALMS 22:1–4

I will say this: because these experiences I had were so tremendous, God was afraid I might be puffed up by them; so I was given a physical condition which has been a thorn in my flesh, a messenger from Satan to hurt and bother me, and prick my pride. Three different times I begged God to make me well again.
Each time he said, "No. But I am with you; that is all you need. My power shows up best in weak people." Now I am glad to boast about how weak I am; I am glad to be a living demonstration of Christ's power, instead of showing off my own power and abilities.   2 CORINTHIANS 12:7–9

And even when you do ask you don't get it because your whole aim is wrong—you want only what will give *you* pleasure.
                                               JAMES 4:3

Don't be impatient for the Lord to act! Keep traveling steadily along his pathway and in due season he will honor you with every blessing, and you will see the wicked destroyed.
                                               PSALMS 37:34

We Are Being Judged

CHECK UP on yourselves. Are you really Christians? Do you pass the test? Do you feel Christ's presence and power more and more within you? Or are you just preteding to be Christians when actually you aren't at all? I hope you can agree that I have stood that test and truly belong to the Lord.

I pray that you will live good lives, not because that will be a feather in our caps, proving that what we teach is right; no, for we want you to do right even if we ourselves are despised. Our responsibility is to encourage the right at all times, not to hope for evil. We are glad to be weak and despised if you are really strong. Our greatest wish and prayer is that you will become mature Christians.   2 CORINTHIANS 13:5–9

Only God's Will

Cling tightly to your faith in Christ and always keep your conscience clear, doing what you know is right. For some people have disobeyed their consciences and have deliberately done what they knew was wrong. It isn't surprising that soon they lost their faith in Christ after defying God like that.

1 TIMOTHY 1:19

You are free from the law, but that doesn't mean you are free to do wrong. Live as those who are free to do only God's will at all times.

1 PETER 2:16

Pray for us, for our conscience is clear and we want to keep it that way.

HEBREWS 13:18

My conscience is clear, but even that isn't final proof. It is the Lord himself who must examine me and decide.

1 CORINTHIANS 4:4

Trust the Promises

God is our refuge and strength, a tested help in times of trouble. And so we need not fear even if the world blows up, and the mountains crumble into the sea. Let the oceans roar and foam; let the mountains tremble!   PSALMS 46:1–3

For the Holy Spirit, God's gift, does not want you to be afraid of people, but to be wise and strong, and to love them and enjoy being with them.   2 TIMOTHY 1:7

We need have no fear of someone who loves us perfectly; his perfect love for us eliminates all dread of what he might do to us. If we are afraid, it is for fear of what he might do to us, and shows that we are not fully convinced that he really loves us. So you see, our love for him comes as a result of his loving us first.   1 JOHN 4:18, 19

But when I am afraid, I will put my confidence in you. Yes, I will trust the promises of God. And since I am trusting him, what can mere man do to me?   PSALMS 56:3, 4

May I
Do My Part

WHEN I AM with the Jews I seem as one of them so that they will listen to the Gospel and I can win them to Christ. When I am with Gentiles who follow Jewish customs and ceremonies I don't argue, even though I don't agree, because I want to help them. When with the heathen I agree with them as much as I can, except of course that I must always do what is right as a Christian. And so, by agreeing, I can win their confidence and help them too.

When I am with those whose consciences bother them easily, I don't act as though I know it all and don't say they are foolish; the result is that they are willing to let me help them. Yes, whatever a person is like, I try to find common ground with him so that he will let me tell him about Christ and let Christ save him. I do this to get the Gospel to them and also for the blessing I myself receive when I see them come to Christ.

1 CORINTHIANS 9:20–23